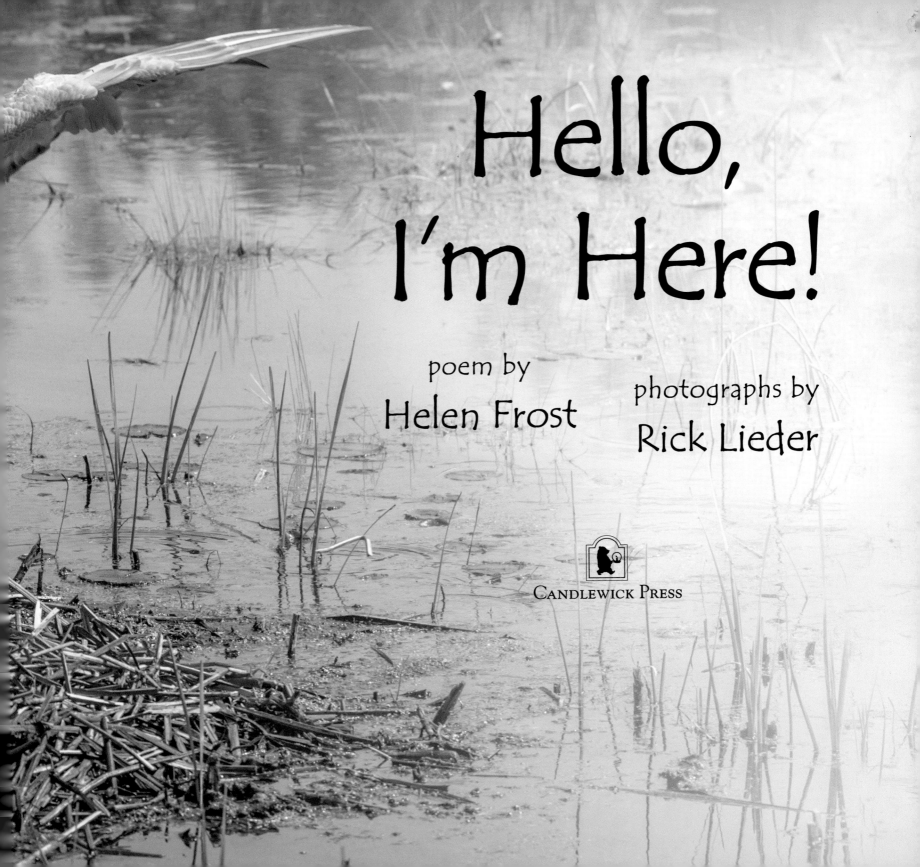

Hello, I'm Here!

poem by
Helen Frost

photographs by
Rick Lieder

CANDLEWICK PRESS

It's getting crowded

inside this egg.

I can't flap a wing

or stretch out a leg.

Who's talking to me?

Is it night or day?

I start to peck,

and my shell falls away.

I'm out in the world—

I don't know where.

Mama? Papa?

Hello, I'm here!

Could I stand up straight and tall?

Will my legs hold me?

What if I fall?

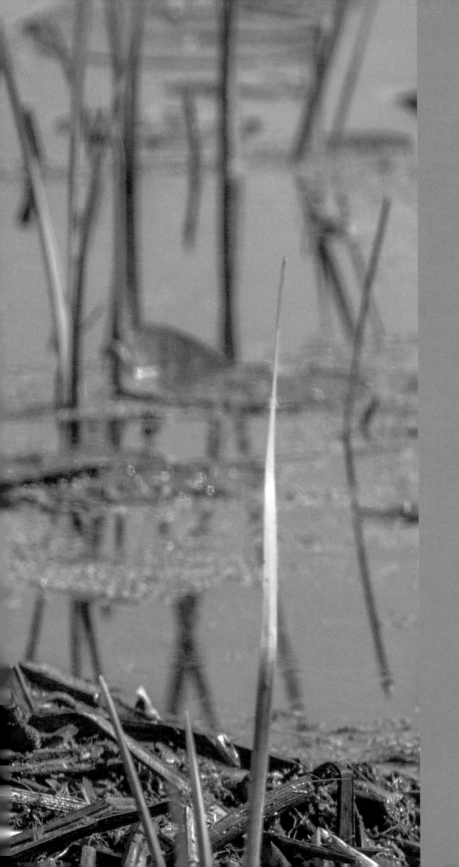

Look, I'm standing!

One step. Another.

Hey, who's this?

Are you my brother?

He walks away.

Wait! I'm coming too.

I might be small,

but I'm following you!

We flap our wings.

We try to dance.

Let's go swimming—

here's our chance!

What made that splash?

Jump in and see.

No! Snapping turtles!

Stay close to me.

Mama, I'm hungry.

What can I eat?

Here's a bug for
your supper.

There's a snail for a treat.

Hundreds of voices

fill the sky.

How did those birds

learn to fly?

We've been busy—

Time for a rest!

Mama's strong wings

make a soft, warm nest.

Sandhill Crane Families

Sandhill cranes nest in marshy places and usually lay two eggs at a time. For about a month, the parents take turns keeping the eggs warm, standing on long spindly legs and leaning down to turn the eggs with their beaks. While still inside their eggs, the chicks make small sounds, and the parents answer.

One egg hatches a few days before the other, and that chick will be a little bigger as they grow. On the first day it is hatched, a chick learns to walk and sometimes to swim. The parents feed the chicks seeds, grains, and insects. Soon the chicks learn to find their own food, including small animals such as snails, lizards, and frogs.

During their first month, the chicks run around and flap their wings as they explore. At night, they sleep under their mother's wings. In their second month, they begin learning to dance, and their wings keep growing. When they are fully grown, their wing-span will be more than six feet.

The young chicks face many dangers. Raccoons and foxes might eat the eggs or the chicks. Snapping turtles might pull the swimming chicks underwater.

By the time they are three months old, sandhill cranes have the feathers they need to fly and long legs like their parents. At this point they are called colts instead of chicks. They practice flying so that when summer is over, they will be ready to migrate south with their parents. Hundreds of sandhill crane families will fly together, filling the air with their calls.

They will return each spring. In a few years, the young cranes will be ready to start families of their own. As they form groups and look for a mate, they will dance by leaping into the air, bobbing their heads up and down, and stretching their wings. Most crane pairs will stay together for the rest of their lives, which can be twenty to thirty years.

For the People of the Crane: present and future generations of Myaamia families. And for Naomi Marie and Kajsa Jean.
H. F.

For everyone at the start of their journey . . . And for Kathe.
R. L.